AF483240

Scapegoating

Oversimplification of Suffering by Blame Shifting and Displacement

Loran Joly

ReEnvision Press

Contents

Preface

This is what one might call a White Paper, or Musing, too, or Rough Draft, ...

And thus, is not Polished; or Utterly-Complete; and too, of course, both a Hypothesis and is Subject to Revision and Change of Mind.

And, too, given the probability of a car accident, or stroke, or heart attack, or cancer, or Alzheimers striking me, ...

Chapter One

The Scriptural Prophet May Be The Highly Evolved Person

A scripture in the Christian texts reads, in the King James version, "A prophet is not without honor except in his own country, among his own relatives, and in his own house."

Mark 6:40

***

I will also state that mankind has had a long history of the concept of a scapegoat, and I'll just mention a few things, including this book on it: "Scapegoat: a History of Blaming Other People", by Charlie Campbell.

And secondly, I will mention what a 95-year-old friend told me once: That "Every family has a black sheep".

I will thirdly state my own experience in the affirmative to this, and secondly regarding somebody I dated for 10 years having experienced the same thing too.

Fourthly there is plenty of material on the internet as YouTube shows on the concept of scapegoating.

Fifthly, I'd make mention the concept of splitting in psychology, which involves seeing things as All or Nothing.

And sixthly, I'd make mention of four personality types pointed out in a book entitled "I'm OK – You're OK", by Thomas Harris.

And in this book, the author talks of his idea of there being two kingpin orientations, one of either the belief that they themselves are always perfect and any pains they experience in life, physically or emotionally, are other people's fault: hence the phrase "I'm okay and you're not okay".

And then they're being the opposing kingpin viewpoint held by a many a person, of "I'm not okay but you are okay": in other words, "Everyone else is okay but me"!

And seventhly, I'd make mention, a spiritual coach who, in an online course, has brought up the concept of people having a default position: I believe that she was talking about this very issue, but she didn't go into extreme detail about it, in the course, that is.

Chapter Two

The Scapegoater Likely Seeks to Get the Other Person to Believe They Are "Junk"

There are also some good articles on the web about scapegoating and what to do about it.

And, I would state my belief that the scapegoat not only wishes to justify in their own mind that they are perfect - no matter what pains they experience.

And that their pains come from an *outside* source, always.

And secondly, they make a very strong attempt to get the scapegoated person to believe this.

So that their incorrect claim will be validated by the very person they are scapegoating, thus perpetuating it all the more.

And depending on the extent to which there are ready sources from a number of people in that particular society that might vet such incorrect rationalizations, it can be very very hard, I believe, for the scapegoated person to fight this off.

Especially if they are not in some manner empowered from breaking free of contact with certain key people doing this to them.

Or also if they have been placed on psychiatric medications which so dull their mind that they really can't think straight or access certain key emotions, such as strong fear or anger.

Chapter Three

Why a Person Likely Believes the Scapegoating Messages

At this point in time, I would state my belief that the word prophet, in scriptural documents typically, and not in common parlance use these days, probably ties directly to a concept of a prophet being a *highly evolved* person.

But alas, as my personal experience and observations, in general, seem to indicate, as well as reading on the matter, I believe the typical highly evolved person in a very toxic family or culture or town will find themselves behind the eight ball, so to speak, earlier in life, and often be rather naive about what you might call human nature in some people.

And all the more so, given that some people, including scape-goaters, are likely very adept at concealing certain key ideas and ways of life and facts in general – almost like operating on a need-to-know basis concerning facts, and getting quite distraught in fact, if their group has a member that reveals anything you might call a secret about the one person in that group.

Such that the cat is then out of the bag about that person's true orientation in certain manners.

And I believe it is further compounded by the reality that an *evolved* younger or older person is going to shy away from using toxic words to symbolize, so to speak, various characteristics of people.

And hence will not be what you call a good observer, except on an intuitive level.

Thus they would likely be very inept at what you might call *winnowing* the good from the bad, however, you're going to define that.

Because they don't want to use terminology that is hateful or blameful in general.

It would grate against their conscience and their calmness and relative non-angry demeanor.

And in order, then, to cope with certain toxic people without being able to winnow them very well, they may find themselves either capitulating in submission or isolating: or both, given circumstances and opportunities.

Chapter Four

The Origins of The Highly Talented Person / "Prophet"

Now I believe the origins of such an individual – the scapegoated person – who shines in their family or town, has certain key aspects:

Such as having had more trauma than average; or, being the one individual amongst many, to seek out therapy or psychoanalysis, receive rather good quality treatment, or at least hang in there, and evolve to better and better treatment.

Or they may have unusually high IQs and be able to process many things that some can't, for that matter.

Or they may have a lot more time on hand than many others because they can't get work due to the stigmatization of being a scapegoat.

Or they have some kind of handicap that many consider off-putting – some might call it "ugly" – and then the person.

Especially if their moral code or empathy level won't let them I do whatever it takes to make a considerable amount of money.

Or if they do not have some key allies, to include perhaps, what you call a relationship that is mostly a business relationship.

They may also have stumbled across someone in their life, in what you could call an accident, who sets them straight on certain matters, or who gave them an unusually high level of acceptance/love.

And this is rather unusual to find.

Or the person may have at one point moved away from the family or town and developed new viewpoints that the others didn't.

And finally, the person may have been of a certain birth order such that they got more quality love, if you will, than the other persons in the family...

And then it had a snowball effect, in time.

Chapter Five

How Does the Scapegoater React to Losing Their Scapegoat?

So my contention then, is that when the person who was once what you call naive about being a scapegoated person then starts to grow out of this, or massively did grow out of it almost completely, the family and town would tend to fill the following to be true, I strongly believe, now:

1. First I believe they are going to feel shame and guilt over the painful effects toward the scapegoated person, for years or even decades both emotionally and sometimes even physically.

2. And this will then clash with their desire to have high self-esteem, based upon the conception in part of their

brain that they are highly loving people who deserve reciprocation from at least some others at a key point of life.

3. But they are now confronted with almost undeniable data that their former beliefs were often a fabrication or rationalization of sorts - call it what you will. And they have then a collapse of sorts, in their self-esteem.

4. Next, I believe the kingpin issue too once the so-called scapegoated person breaks free, the others will tend to feel envy: i.e. they're going to realize that this person has basically broken free of so much, and that he or she is so much happier than they..

5. And compounded by the reality that they probably will not be able to do the same thing unless that scapegoated person can somehow pass on particular key training – rather unlikely.

6. So the person who was doing the scapegoating, or the town doing the scapegoating, or the family doing the scapegoating, is going to feel quite stuck.

7. And this is going to be a very painful feeling indeed. And it may even drive them to substance abuse like

alcoholism.

8. Next, the scapegoating persons are going to realize they lost their scapegoat, and now will have to put in a lot of effort to find/create a new one: which is a pain in the neck, they're going to think.

9. And then there is the concern amongst the scapegoats who lost their scapegoat, that they have now been found out, so to speak. And they may have stark fear - even call it paranoia if you will - regarding possible counter damages for the past: to include bodily in nature.

10. And then too, there may be concern, surely, that the person's reputation might be damaged, especially on-line, and this then impacts how they go about life in their community, or how they would earn money and ancillary comments that might be made on the internet or in books also.

11. They might even fear what you would call counter-actions in a court of law.

12. Or perhaps they may fear a memoir coming out.

Chapter Six

Attempts to Keep The Scapegoat "In Place"

And so I tend to see these things as playing out in several possible scenarios, either the scapegoating person continually seeking to bait the scapegoated person into anger, or a comment made that is disrespectful and in return then, a tit-for-tat continuing on.

Secondly, the person who was once the scapegoat may isolate from the scapegoated person of the past so as not to incur any possible counter comments or have their conscience jogged if you will, or maybe I should say, their self-esteem rather denigrated in their own mind – lowered, shall we say.

And if the scenarios above do not happen, I believe the person then may find themselves having to swallow a bitter pill and make a starkly honest apology for the past, or they may have a mental breakdown.

And short of that they may turn to substance abuse or other coping mechanisms to block their own mental pain over the whole thing.

This letter point is brought up admirably, I believe, by Robert Greene in a very short video about Anton Chekov the writer, noting how Anton Chekov pulled way ahead of his family, and they in turn descended into alcoholism and other negative toxic aspects of life.

Chapter Seven

How Does a Society Contribute to Scapegoating?

I would close by mentioning observations I have made, as well as reading I've done, particularly in Dr. Anne Schaeff's book, "When Society Become's an Addict", noting that Anne Schaeff was a Cherokee Indian who passed away a few years ago:

I close if this is also echoed by the psychologist Dr. Romani, who originally grew up in India. She in fact states that this one issue is something that makes her blood boil.

Dedication

To my parents, who made this possible.

For instance, my mother, an immigrant from eastern Poland, having come to America at the age of twelve, after a two week long boat journey, to Ellis Island....

My mother as a young gal in Europe, before coming to America

And to my father, too, a most astute Trainer in life....

Brought up in the ghettos of Philadelphia; left school at the age of seventeen; and later acquired a GED and went on to obtain a Ph.D. degree at a major University in English Literature; who thus led to my interest and pursuit of writing at a very early age; and too, with respect to his love of photography, both of these areas, too, rubbing off on me: hence, "The apple doesn't fall far from the tree"?

Training!

Then, too, my grandparents:

For significantly, my grandmother raised me during my first four years, in my waking hours. And her husband – my grandfather – worked in the tool and die industry for cars; she, born in eastern Poland, like my mother, and was a farmer there; he, born in Odessa, Ukraine, and a Mennonite, and herb-collector and maker of many grandfather clocks in his spare time, on their farm in Michigan:

Grandparents in Niagara Falls

And to my farm experience, as a youth, each summer, in Michigan:

Then, too, to a man of great impact upon myself, too, from the ages of twelve to fourteen, starting when I first sought him out to help me obtain a ham radio license at that age of twelve:

Mr. Foster; who interestingly did have a foster child he raised when I knew him; he helped me obtain my ham license; he hunted; he took me to ham conventions and camped with me; he collected stamps and coins; and let me build electronic projects in his workshop; and even took me for a ride on his motorcycle, popping a wheelie

About the Author

The author resides in Kentucky,

and welcomes comments at message@goldpogo.com

Author, Mt Mitchell, North Carolina 2023

Author a few years back...

Refund policy

Refund information:

If for any reason, you find this item not quite your cup of tea, I am most happy to provide a refund, no questions asked.

One can contact me at message@goldpogo.com.

Or, one can write me at this address, asking for a refund:

Loran Joly

Box # 1036

1303 US 127 South

Suite 104

Frankfort, KY 40601

www.ingramcontent.com/pod-product-compliance
Lightning Source LLC
Chambersburg PA
CBHW040214130726
47973CB00057B/122

* 9 7 9 8 3 3 0 3 5 0 0 1 8 *